HAT!
A Vaudeville

Book and lyrics by
John Strand
Music by
Dennis McCarthy

Based on the 1851 French play
AN ITALIAN STRAW HAT
by Eugène Labiche

BROADWAY PLAY PUBLISHING INC
New York
www.broadwayplaypublishing.com
info@broadwayplaypublishing.com

First printing: July 2011
I S B N: 978-0-88145-466-6

Back cover photo courtesy of South Coast Rep
Book design: Marie Donovan
Page make-up: Adobe Indesign
Typeface: Palatino
Printed and bound in the U S A

HAT! A VAUDEVILLE, a translation-adaptation of Eugène Labiche's 1851 vaudeville farce, UN CHAPEAU DE PAILLE D'ITALIE (AN ITALIAN STRAW HAT), was commissioned by South Coast Repertory, Costa Mesa, California.

HAT! A VAUDEVILLE premiered at South Coast Repertory, on 14 September 2008. The cast and creative contributors were as follows:

FADLEY	Daniel Blinkoff
HELEN	Erika Whalen
NONCORT	Richard Doyle
BOBBY	Matthew Koehler
ANAIS, BARONESS DE CHAMPIGNY	Michelle Duffy
EMILE, NISNARDI	Damon Kirsche
UNCLE FEZ, VISCOUNT VON ROMANOV	Patrick Kerr
VIRGINIA, CLARA	Melissa van der Schyff
FELIX, BEAUPERTHUIS	Alan Blumenfeld
TARDIVEAU, FARNSWORTH	Kasey Mahaffy

Director	Stefan Novinski
Musical direction	Dennis Castellano
Choreography	Christine Kellogg
Set design	Donna Marquet
Costumes	Shigeru Yaji
Lighting	Lonnie Rafael Alcaraz
Dramaturgy	Megan Monaghan

The production included the following instruments, played by five musicians: piano, acoustic bass, drums/light percussion, woodwinds (doubling flute, piccolo and clarinet), trumpet (Bb and C).

CHARACTERS & SETTING

FELIX, *a domestic*
VIRGINIA, *a domestic*
UNCLE FEZ, FADLEY's *elderly uncle*
FADLEY, *about to be married*
HELEN, *his bride-to-be*
NONCORT, *the father-in-law*
BOBBY, HELEN's *amorous cousin*
ANAIS, *a married woman*
EMILE, *a soldier*
CLARA, *hat shop owner*
TARDIVEAU, *a sales clerk*
BARONESS DE CHAMPIGNY
VISCOUNT VON ROMANOV
FARNSWORTH, *a servant*
NISNARDI, *a famous opera singer*
BEAUPERTHUIS, *a wronged husband*

WEDDING GUESTS, *two or three silent roles, are optional.*

The play takes place in New York City, circa 1906.

HAT! A VAUDEVILLE requires a minimum cast of ten actors, three women and seven men. They play a total of 16 roles.

The actors required & suggested distribution of roles:

Actor 1. Male, mid-30s: FADLEY

Actor 2. Female, 20s: HELEN

Actor 3. Male, 50s: NONCORT

Actor 4. Male, 30: BOBBY

Actor 5. Male, 50s: UNCLE FEZ; VISCOUNT

Actor 6. Male 40s: FELIX; BEAUPERTHUIS

Actor 7. Female, 20s: VIRGINIA; CLARA

Actor 8. Female, 30s: ANAIS; BARONESS

Actor 9. Male, late 30s: EMILE; NISNARDI

Actor 10. Male, 20s: TARDIVEAU; FARNSWORTH

ACKNOWLEDGEMENTS

Our thanks to David Emmes, Martin Benson and John Glore of South Coast Repertory for their support during the development of this project, and for their expertise in putting together the team that produced the final product on stage. Thanks, too, to Stefan Novinski for his skill, enthusiasm and intelligence, qualities rivaled only by his patience. A special thanks to Megan Monaghan for her unwavering support, astute observations both musical and textual, and her resolute cheerfulness throughout. And finally, our undying gratitude to the actors and the creative team for the joyous spirit that illuminated the whole process. It was a privilege and a true pleasure to work with them, all.

— John Strand and Dennis McCarthy

FOREWORD

A conservative, acquisitive middle class, intensely interested in financial aggrandizement, carefully protective of the status quo. Prosperity, rapid growth, wild speculation in the stock market. A deep distrust of foreigners and foreign influence. The compelling topics of the day are money, property, fashion and entertainment.

This was the world Eugène Labiche lived in and wrote about, Second Empire France, 1848-1870.

Eugène Labiche (1815-1888) raised the popular form of vaudeville to a level of social portraiture equal to the great satirists, from Molière to Thornton Wilder. A dozen of the 175 plays he wrote have remained perennial favorites on European stages for a century and a half. He is rarely performed in the United States, however. "Too French" is the usual charge.

Labiche is recognized as a master of comic plot and action, two essential traits of "high" vaudeville (the genre can be generally described as fast-moving comic farce with songs). But of equal interest are his razor-sharp portraits of a self-satisfied middle class whose elaborate schemes to advance its own financial or social positions form the basis of his best plays. He sketches his characters with humor and understanding, but above all with accuracy.

Labiche managed to enjoy popular, critical and financial success in his career. He was elected to the Académie Française in 1880.

His play AN ITALIAN STRAW HAT opened in Paris on Aug. 14, 1851 at the Palais-Royal, one of the city's best vaudeville venues. The theater manager was so certain the play was going to fail that he left town the morning of the opening, unable to witness the disaster. But the play was an enormous success. Publicity was much enhanced by the fact that during a performance one of the spectators, a corpulent gentlemen, collapsed choking in the aisle and was carried from the theater. He had died laughing.

The original, like the vaudeville model popular through the latter half of the 19th century, included music and song. The songs were popular tunes of the day, well known to the audience. Labiche and one of his collaborators (he seldom worked alone) rewrote the lyrics, usually comic. Americans should recognize the genre: it is the direct ancestor of George Kaufman's scripts for the Marx Brothers films, among other 20th century classics.

The present version is an adaptation, set in New York at the turn of the 20th century, and features new music and new lyrics. I have taken many liberties with the text, but I have tried throughout to be faithful to the spirit of the original. This version is meant as a loving homage to Eugène Labiche and the High Vaudeville style he was instrumental in establishing a century and a half ago.

John Strand, Washington, DC

For Amanda

Prologue

(Lights come up on the parading entrance of a group of six model citizens belonging to the time and place, New York City, the late Gilded Age, circa 1906. A pleasant, handsome-looking bunch, one notices right away. Very nicely dressed, too, with the proper accessories: parasols or canes, and of course, their hats. The six are divided for the moment into three distinct groups: a wedding party, consisting of HELEN, *the bride,* NONCORT, *her father, and* BOBBY, *her cousin; then a loving couple,* ANAIS *and her friend and protector,* EMILE; *and finally our protagonist and leading man,* FADLEY... *Inspired perhaps by the beauty and promise of the day, or even a deep, well-fed satisfaction with the world as they have carefully arranged it, they address us in song.)*

FADLEY: What, you may inquire,
Is the thing we most desire
In this life?

ALL: This happy life.
Our perfect life!
This happy life!

ANAIS: What, you may well query,
According to our theory
Makes this life

ALL: This happy life.
Our perfect life!
This happy life!

FADLEY: Is it love? Is it wealth?
The golden glow of robust health?

NONCOURT, HELEN, BOBBY:
Is it fame? Or success?
The utter absence of all stress?

ANAIS: Respectability.
A place in high society.

ALL: All these things in measure
Combine to give us pleasure
In this life
This happy life
Our perfect life!
This happy life!

FADLEY: There is one item though
No happy person can forego.

ANAIS: It is a declaration
A stylistic exclamation

HELEN: A vital choice you make
A thing never to forsake:

ALL: It's your hat!
Yes, your hat.
There's no arguing with that.

FADLEY: It elevates and designates,

ANAIS: Fashion-wise, identifies
The owner's social class, sir.

ALL WOMEN: To be without is a disaster!

HELEN: It's your halo, it's your crown,
What heaven sees when it looks down.

ALL: God save your hat!
Yes, your hat!
There's no replacing that!

(Dramatic piano)

FADLEY: But what if tragedy occurred?

ANAIS: This happy life? Don't be absurd.

FADLEY: What if...just let me posit:
What if a lady lost it?
Suppose it came to pass
That a certain lady's hat
Should suddenly
Tragically
Be gone?

(ANAIS's *hat disappears into the flies. Panic: a
practically naked woman!*)

ANAIS: My hat!!

NONCOURT, BOBBY: A naked woman!

EMILE: Good God! Put something on!

NONCORT: What was that evil force, sir?

FADLEY: I hate to say it, but...my horse, sir.

ALL: Your horse!

EMILE: You cad!

ALL: An attack on her propriety!
Oh hatless! Such anxiety!
Do the Christian thing, sir.
Relief to the lady, bring, sir!
Uneasy lies the head without its crown!

(*They surround and attack* FADLEY *with their hats*)

ALL: (*Angrily, at* FADLEY)
Find her hat!
Yes, her hat!
There's no arguing with that!

FADLEY: (*Under attack*) All right, all right, I will...!
But...!

NONCORT: But?

EMILE: But?

ANAIS: But?

FADLEY: In a Vaudeville tale
Best-laid plans can sometimes fail.

ANAIS, EMILE: *(Considering it)* What?
(Dismissing it)

No, never.
Not in this life!

ALL:
This happy life?   Find that hat!
Our perfect life?   Go find that hat!
This happy life?   She needs that hat!

This happy life!!   Find that hat!

(The song ends and the happy participants scramble in a panic for the exits…)

(But two figures remain, on opposite sides of the stage: our hero FADLEY and his bride-to-be, HELEN. They discover one another…then come together and embrace for this unchaperoned, stolen moment)

HELEN: Winslow.

FADLEY: Helen.

HELEN: "Winnie."

FADLEY: "Hellie."

HELEN: My little "Win."

FADLEY: My little "Hell." That doesn't sound right.

HELEN: Just a few more hours—

FADLEY: A mere couple of hundred minutes—

HELEN: And we'll belong to each other forever.

FADLEY: I am the luckiest man in Manhattan.

HELEN: Are you scared?

FADLEY: Me?

HELEN: You've been a bachelor for so long.

FADLEY: Not *that* long.

HELEN: Papa says you're not the marrying kind.

FADLEY: He doesn't know how much I love you.

HELEN: Loving's easy, he says. Marriage, that's the hard part. I hope you're ready, Winslow.

FADLEY: Darling, of course I am. I bought you that engagement ring, didn't I?

HELEN: My cousin was engaged——till she caught her fiancé with another woman, right in his own apartment!

FADLEY: That's horrible. She broke it off?

HELEN: No, just fractured it.

FADLEY: Ow.

HELEN: The man still walks with a limp.

(Music...)

HELEN: It's going to be very different for us.

FADLEY: Good. Very different how?

(A bride-to-be has a right to sing; HELEN exercises it)

> HELEN: If we
> Keep it simple, make it clear
> Speak our hearts and be sincere,
> We've got a chance
>
> If we
> Don't deceive, reject the lies,
> See the truth in each other's eyes,
> We've got a chance
>
> HELEN & FADLEY:
> We could be all we want to be,
> If we just start with honesty.
> Trust each other,

Understand
Love and trust go hand-in-hand

FADLEY: If we
Hold each other through the night,
Wish for joy with all our might,

HELEN & FADLEY:
We've got a chance
We've got a chance

(Enter hurriedly the father-in-law, the cantankerous NONCORT, *trailed by the cousin,* BOBBY, *suspicious and confrontational.* NONCORT *breaks up the moment and points* HELEN *to the exit)*

NONCORT: Helen.

HELEN: Yes, Papa.

*(*HELEN *exits.)*

NONCORT: No stepping in the flower beds, Fadley.
You're not married yet.

(Exit NONCORT *and* BOBBY.*)*

FADLEY: Maybe she was secretly adopted.

(Transition music. FADLEY *glances at his watch and hurries off to continue his fateful day…)*

ACT ONE

(*The tastelessly furnished townhouse of our hero* FADLEY, *a young man who, through a combination of pure luck and a shallow, materialistic nature, has recently done well speculating in the markets. But he's a likeable sort nonetheless. The set features the requisite double doors, center; separate doors to the left and to the right of these; and entrances at both wings, downstage.* FADLEY *is momentarily absent. Instead we have* VIRGINIA, *a housemaid, and* FELIX, *a domestic servant. The latter is amorously mugging the former*)

VIRGINIA: Would you stop? ...I'm not here to play games... Felix! Get off me!

FELIX: One little kiss?

VIRGINIA: No.

FELIX: Virginia. We're from the same hometown.

VIRGINIA: What, I have to kiss everybody from Garden City, New Jersey? You promised to show me the wedding presents. Your master is getting married at noon. Hurry up.

FELIX: Relax. Mister Fadley went for his morning ride. We're alone, Ginnie.

(*An attempted embrace;* VIRGINIA *ducks* FELIX.)

VIRGINIA: So tell me about the bride. Is she pretty?

FELIX: Better. She's rich. The father owns a nursery.

VIRGINIA: There's money in babies?

FELIX: Plants, Sweetheart.

VIRGINIA: Felix, if the new bride needs a domestic, mention my name?

FELIX: You're leaving your household?

VIRGINIA: I can't talk about it.

FELIX: Come on, Ginnie.

VIRGINIA: No. I never criticize my employers.

(A beat)

The mean, lying, tight-fisted old toad! And his *wife*! The minute the old man leaves the house, bam, she's out the door. And where does she go?

FELIX: Where?

VIRGINIA: She refuses to say.

FELIX: Ginnie. You can't stay in a household that shuns the moral values of this great nation. You let me see what I can work out here.

VIRGINIA: Will you, Felix? You know… I always wanted to serve with someone from my hometown.

FELIX: "Garden City: Jersey's Little Paradise."

(Moved by nostalgia for their paradise lost, they sing.)

> FELIX: Garden City
> VIRGINIA: Just too pretty
> FELIX: Head and shoulders far above
> VIRGINIA: A boy and girl can fall in love
> FELIX: It's itty-bitty
> Garden City
> VIRGINIA: A very Paris to us somehow
> FELIX & VIRGINIA:
> What a pity
> What a pity

What a pity
We're not there right now

(VIRGINIA *lets* FELIX *kiss her… After a beat, enter a well-dressed, loveable-looking older gent,* UNCLE FEZ, *carrying a large wedding present, wrapped)*

UNCLE FEZ: Good morning, servants. Where is the wedding party?

FELIX: Gone to the wedding, you old buzzard.

VIRGINIA: Hey!

FELIX: It's the uncle. Deaf as a post. Hey, relic: time for a memory lapse?

UNCLE FEZ: Why, yes, don't mind if I do. Here, Sweetie, put this with the other presents, would you?

(UNCLE FEZ *hands the present to* VIRGINIA.)

VIRGINIA: Sure, Grandpa. Hey, you're cute. Are you rich, by any chance?

UNCLE FEZ: Oh yes, Dear. But I'm taking medication for it.

FELIX: *(Heading her toward an exit)* The kitchen. I'll be right along.

(FELIX *and* UNCLE FEZ *watch* VIRGINIA *strut off.)*

UNCLE FEZ: What a lovely little bottom.

FELIX: At your age, you old letch?

UNCLE FEZ: I think I feel the blood flowing. When does the ceremony begin, young man?

FELIX: It's canceled. The bride ran off with the stable boy.

UNCLE FEZ: Good, good.

FELIX: You're on your own, Moses. I got a present to unwrap.

UNCLE FEZ: Fine idea. Cream, with a shot of brandy.

FELIX: Family full of nutcakes.

UNCLE FEZ: No cake for me, thanks. Horrible constipation.

(Exit FELIX)

UNCLE FEZ: What a pleasant young servant. Where is my nephew?

(Enter FADLEY.)

FADLEY: Uncle Fez?

UNCLE FEZ: Congratulations, my lad, on this glorious occasion, et cetera.

FADLEY: Aren't you a bit early?

UNCLE FEZ: No, no, your servant's getting me one.

FADLEY: You won't believe this, Uncle: I was out for a ride this morning—

UNCLE FEZ: Your bride?

FADLEY: No, my horse.

UNCLE FEZ: That seems a bit harsh, Winslow.

FADLEY: So there we were in Central Park—

UNCLE FEZ: *(Shaking his hand)* Of *course* I brought the wedding present.

FADLEY: Yes, thank you, Uncle. And I dropped my new riding crop—cost me twelve dollars—so I dismount and suddenly, the horse takes off like a shot—

UNCLE FEZ: Just a small one. Nothing too strong before noon.

FADLEY: When I finally catch up to him, he's standing next to a lilac bush, eating a woman's hat.

UNCLE FEZ: Constipation.

FADLEY: "Constipation"?

UNCLE FEZ: You suffer from it too?

FADLEY: So out of the bushes step this woman and a soldier. She left her stupid hat hanging from a tree branch. And what were they doing in the bushes?

UNCLE FEZ: Waiting, my boy.

FADLEY: Huh?

UNCLE FEZ: Patience is the golden rule of the stock market.

FADLEY: Oh, damn, I forgot. You're deaf.

UNCLE FEZ: Really? That's terrible news.

FADLEY: *(His pocket watch)* Oh, no. It's almost noon!

(Perhaps it's the pressure, but FADLEY *suddenly resorts to song.* UNCLE FEZ *joins him.)*

> FADLEY: My hour now is nearing.
> Dear uncle hard of hearing,
> Try to stay out of my way.

> UNCLE FEZ: I'm eagerly awaiting,
> So stop procrastinating,
> I haven't got all day.

> For I have cleavage yet to glimpse,
> Lovely bottoms still to pinch,
> Young maidens to convince.

> FADLEY: I'm glad someone's having fun
> While my nerves are come undone.
> Have you seen my cummerbund!?

UNCLE FEZ: Of course! But you want to add a raw egg.

> FADLEY, UNCLE FEZ:
> And no more horses eating hats
> Please!
> No horses eating hats!

*(*UNCLE FEZ *shuffles off toward the kitchen and exits.)*

FADLEY: *(Calling)* Felix!

(Enter FELIX*)*

FADLEY: Did you finish the bridal bathroom yet?

FELIX: It's tough going, Mr. Fadley. A lot of your water pipes are crammed full of water.

FADLEY: Can't you hurry it up? I'm getting married in an hour.

FELIX: Mister Fadley, you need a female domestic.

FADLEY: What for?

FELIX: Your new wife, she can't be laying out her own nightclothes. I've got just the girl to solve your problem.

FADLEY: One problem at a time. Right now I have to go get married. Here, do something with this.

*(*FADLEY *hands* FELIX *the fragment of straw hat, then exits.)*

(Enter VIRGINIA.*)*

VIRGINIA: So what did he say?

FELIX: Felix, he says to me, you advise me to hire the girl, she's hired.

VIRGINIA: Oh, Felix! When do I start?

FELIX: After the reference check and a physical.

VIRGINIA: I have to see a doctor?

FELIX: No, I can do it.

VIRGINIA: You?

FELIX: Do you know how far I went in medical school before I decided to specialize in butlering? Open your mouth. Stick out your tongue. You better come with me.

VIRGINIA: Is something wrong?

FELIX: It might be nothing at all. But then again…

*(*FELIX *exits,* VIRGINIA *follows.)*

VIRGINIA: Felix. What did you see?

(*Exit* VIRGINIA. *Enter* FADLEY, *in the final stages of putting on his tux… Underscoring throughout his spoken lines*)

FADLEY: One hour left…then it's over. I'll turn into a married man. With a wife…

I'll be married.
It sounds so very
Safe and sane.
How can I complain?
That's more or less how life is meant to be.
I'll have a wife. A family.
And I'll be
Happy.

The words "I do"
Commit me to
A faithful heart.
Till death do us part?
That's more or less how marriage has to be.
I'll have a wife. Fidelity.
And I'll be
Happy.

(*Spoken*) It's time to grow up and have a bright future. With a father–in–law. "Money doesn't grow on trees, it grows *because* of trees!" If I hear that one more time, I'm going to spit on his hydrangeas.

You'll say it's only
Matrimony
I won't be lonely anymore.

I love her dearly
I see it clearly
In a year she'll be with child?

And so will I.

I forgot about that.

(Spoken) This is no time to get cold feet. I've had my flings. There was Gwendolyn. And Louisa. And Clara. *(Recalling it)* Ouch. But that's all in the past now.

> It's time I wed
> At last I shed
> My wastrel ways
> For golden days
> That's more or less how life is meant to be.
> I'll have responsibility.
> And I'll be…happy.
> If it kills me.
> I'll be happy.

(A knock on the door)

This is it.
(It's painful, but he manages to get to the door, put on a forced smile, and open)
Darling!

(Enter defiantly a man in a junior officer's uniform)

EMILE: I think not.

(Enter ANAIS behind him, fearfully. She is hatless.)

ANAIS: Emile, I don't want a scene.

EMILE: Sir! I dare say you are surprised to see us.

FADLEY: If this is about a donation to the Wounded Veterans Fund, private—

EMILE: Lieutenant!

FADLEY: *(Attempting to show them out)* –I'm very busy this morning, so if you don't mind—

EMILE: Did you place your bare hand, unauthorized, upon my uniform?

ANAIS: Sir, we are here about a hat.

FADLEY: Oh, it's you. Look, I am really sorry about the hat.

ANAIS: *You* are sorry? *You* have not seen your hat eaten before your very eyes.

EMILE: Your new hat.

ANAIS: Italian straw.

EMILE: With fruit.

ANAIS: A favorite of my husband's.

FADLEY: "Husband"?

ANAIS: That is—I mean to say, my aunt—

FADLEY: There's a husband? You're strolling around the woods with a soldier, madam? Without a hat?

EMILE: What are you insinuating?

ANAIS: I will have you know, sir... *(Searching for it)*

EMILE: She will have you know...

ANAIS: That this gentleman is my cousin.

EMILE: Precisely.

ANAIS: I was advising him.

EMILE: She was advising me.

ANAIS: On his career.

FADLEY: In the bushes? Without a hat?

EMILE: *(Lifting a wooden chair and slamming it to the floor)* I have had enough of your impudence, sir!

FADLEY: Don't you damage my furniture, corporal.

EMILE: Lieutenant!

ANAIS: I hold you responsible, sir, for the eating of my personal property.

FADLEY: I do not eat hats.

EMILE: Your horse, sir—

FADLEY: My horse was within his legal rights.

ANAIS: His what?

FADLEY: And if he suffers from indigestion, expect to hear from my solicitor.

EMILE: *(The chair again)* Sir!

FADLEY: That chair cost six dollars.

EMILE: I demand immediate restitution of the hat belonging to this innocent lady, my cousin!

FADLEY: I tossed you a five-dollar bill to pay for the hat!

ANAIS: *(Withdrawing a dollar-sized piece of paper)* Do you mean this, sir?

FADLEY: *(Caught in the act)* A laundry receipt?

(A knock on the door. The father-in-law's voice, off, calling: "Fadley?")

FADLEY: They're here!

ANAIS: Who?

FADLEY: My wedding party! If Helen and her father find a woman in here—without a hat—!

ANAIS: Trapped—in a stranger's apartment—with a soldier—!

FADLEY: I thought he was your cousin?

EMILE: Get rid of those guests!

FADLEY: Get rid of them?

(The voice, off: "Fadley!")

ANAIS: We'll hide in here.

(EMILE and ANAIS duck into the bedroom, left.)

FADLEY: You can't go in there! That's the honeymoon bedroom!

(FADLEY too dashes into the bedroom.)

(The wedding party enters: NONCORT, *the father;* HELEN, *the bride;* BOBBY, *her affectionate cousin.* NONCORT *carries a potted plant, some manner of flowering bush, apparently.)*

HELEN: Honey?

NONCORT: Fadley?

HELEN: Winslow!

NONCORT: Fadley!

(Only one thing to do: NONCORT *and* BOBBY *sing)*

> NONCOURT, BOBBY:
> We are here and he is not
> This very fact tells us a lot
> About his personality
> His lack of punctuality
>
> His irresponsibility
>
> I bet he hasn't made his bed
> You wouldn't listen when I said
> Call it off

HELEN: Winslow, Honey?

> Call it off
> He's got that stogie-smoker's cough
> His head is hard, his heart is soft

NONCORT: "Fadley." Is that Jewish?

> He'll be shouting Maazeltov!
> Call it off!

(Enter FADLEY.*)*

NONCORT: There you are!

HELEN: Winslow!

FADLEY: Helen, darling.

*(*FADLEY *and* HELEN *move toward one another but* NONCORT *blocks* FADLEY's *path while* BOBBY *blocks*

HELEN's. *Business:* FADLEY *and* HELEN *reaching out, trying unsuccessfully to connect)*

NONCORT: You were supposed to greet us on the street as we arrived with the wedding coaches!

BOBBY: That's the tradition.

HELEN: Winslow…!

FADLEY: Helen, sweetheart…!

NONCORT: I'm paying for all this, at least respect tradition.

HELEN: Winnie, dear!

BOBBY: *Three* coaches.

FADLEY: Helen!

NONCORT: Six horses. Nine dollars and fifty cents an hour. How about respecting *that?*

HELEN: Papa, get out of our way!

NONCORT: Silence! It's not too late to call this off.

HELEN: Papa!

BOBBY: Call it off, Uncle Karl. Think of the money you'd save.

HELEN: Bobby, muzzle it! *(A beat, as she moves to* FADLEY's *side)* I'm the one getting married around here, and *this* is my future husband.

NONCORT: Your future husband can't even observe tradition on his own wedding day.

BOBBY: He doesn't respect us.

FADLEY: That's not true, Cousin Bobby.

BOBBY: It's because we work the soil.

NONCORT: Let me tell you something, Mister Stock Market Speculator: money doesn't grow on trees—it grows *because* of trees.

FADLEY: That's a great one, father-in-law. I'll have to remember that.

HELEN: Tell him about the myrtle, Papa.

NONCORT: Can we just get out of here and get this over with?

HELEN: Tell him, Papa.

NONCORT: Bobby! My myrtle.

(BOBBY *hands* NONCORT *the potted plant.*)

NONCORT: *Laegerstromia indica.* Planted with my own two hands the day my baby girl came into this world of pain and hurt…I'll place it next to her marriage bed…so she'll never forget…how much I love her! *(He is overcome)*

HELEN: Oh, Papa! You're so good!

(They hug. Sobs. FADLEY, *self-conscious at first, tentatively places a hand on* NONCORT's *shoulder.)*

FADLEY: That is really touching.

NONCORT: *(Instantly snapping out of it, violently shaking his foot)* Damn these shoes…!

HELEN: You should have broken them in first, Papa.

NONCORT: There wasn't time.

HELEN: Oh…!

(HELEN *has begun a very un-bride-like twitch and shake of her shoulders, jerking her arms and upper body as she attempts to reach an apparent itch between her shoulder blades.* NONCORT *meanwhile stands on one foot and shakes the other.* BOBBY *joins in with a nervous tic of his own)*

FADLEY: Helen, sweetheart… Does your family have a nervous tic-thing you want to tell me about?

HELEN: Papa.

NONCORT: What is it?

HELEN: I think I have a pin stuck.

BOBBY: Here, let me get it out.

FADLEY: Whoa, there! That's my wife, eventually.

BOBBY: Back off, Snob. We're cousins.

FADLEY: Oh, I know how *that* works!

NONCORT: They've always been affectionate.

FADLEY: That's what I'm talking about!

NONCORT: Go into the other room and get it unstuck.

FADLEY: *(Barring the door to the room where EMILE and ANAIS are hiding)* No! Not in there!

NONCORT: Why not?

FADLEY: Paint! Fresh paint!

NONCORT: Well, don't touch the walls.

FADLEY: No! Fumes, deadly paint fumes!

BOBBY: Wait a minute here. Just what are you hiding in that room, Fadley?

HELEN: Bobby.

BOBBY: No, let him answer. What's behind that door, Snob?

(A beat as they all await an answer)

FADLEY: *(Not able to think of anything more plausible)* A soldier with a temper and a strange woman without a hat?

(A beat…then HELEN bursts out with a loud, shrill laugh, more of a cackle, actually)

HELEN: Oh, Papa! Isn't he funny?

NONCORT: A regular circus clown. Bobby, what time is it?

BOBBY: We're twelve minutes behind schedule. That's an extra dollar-ninety on the carriages.

NONCORT: Bobby, put your cousin in the damn carriage.

> NONCORT & BOBBY:
> Let's get this show on the road
> Let's get this done
>
> HELEN: My heart is convinced
> That he's the one
>
> NONCORT & BOBBY:
> Let's get this over with
> Let's get this done
>
> FADLEY: I'm fighting back the urge
> To cut and run
>
> NONCORT & BOBBY:
> Let's get this show on the road
> Let's get this done
>
> HELEN: My golden journey
> Has just begun!
>
> This is my time
>
> NONCORT, BOBBY, FADLEY:
> Now she finds
>
> HELEN: I can shape
> My future
>
> I won't give in
>
> NONCORT, BOBBY, FADLEY:
> Plans to win
>
> HELEN: And escape
> My family
>
> NONCORT, BOBBY, FADLEY: The duress
> Of family
>
> HELEN: God bless
> My family
> Give me less

Of my family
(Spoken, to the audience)
You see what I mean.

ALL: Let's get this over with
Let's get this done

NONCORT: This farce is costing me
A painful sum

ALL: Let's get this show on the road
Let's get this done!

(As they exit...)

FADLEY: Uh-oh! Almost forgot my gloves. I'll be right along.

(They exit. FADLEY opens the bedroom door, out step EMILE and ANAIS)

FADLEY: Get out of my house immediately!

(Enter from the kitchen, VIRGINIA)

VIRGINIA: Mister Fadley, sir? What do I do with what's left of the lady's straw hat that your horse ate?

(ANAIS screams, hides herself behind EMILE before VIRGINIA can see her)

ANAIS: Emile! My chambermaid!

EMILE: *(To FADLEY)* Get rid of that girl *now!*

FADLEY: What?

EMILE: Now!

FADLEY: *(To VIRGINIA)* You: get out of here! Go!

VIRGINIA: Does this mean I don't get the job?

FADLEY: *(Grabbing the piece of straw hat)* Get! Out!!

(She exits, running)

FADLEY: Who was that person and why did I scream at her? My house is turning into one of those vaudeville farces!

EMILE: *(Trying to revive* ANAIS, *who has almost fainted)* Darling...cousin...

FADLEY: Get her out of here, sergeant.

EMILE: Lieutenant, damn you!

ANAIS: *(Reviving)* Sir, I cannot leave this house!

FADLEY: What?

ANAIS: That was my chambermaid! If she discovers me without my hat—with my cousin—she'll tell my husband!

EMILE: There will be a drama, sir—with firearms.

FADLEY: Firearms? Here?

ANAIS: There's only one hope. Replace that hat.

FADLEY: Good idea. Use the back stairs when you leave.

ANAIS: Impossible. Appear on the street hatless?

EMILE: The woman can barely stand, sir. I will not abandon her in this condition. *You* find the hat.

FADLEY: Me? I have a wedding to go to—mine!

ANAIS: We will not leave these premises without an exact replica of the hat that your animal destroyed.

FADLEY: But I'm coming back here after the wedding—with my wife!

EMILE: Not without that hat, sir.

NONCORT: *(Calling, off)* Fadley!

FADLEY: Oh no.

*(*EMILE *and* ANAIS *duck into the bedroom. Enter* NONCORT.*)*

NONCORT: I heard voices in here.

FADLEY: Just practicing my speech.

NONCORT: What speech?

FADLEY: *(Pushing him back out the door)* Go downstairs, father-in-law, you're making us late.

(FADLEY closes the door on NONCORT. ANAIS emerges from the bedroom door.)

ANAIS: Italian straw. Exact replica.

FADLEY: Don't touch anything while I'm gone!

(NONCORT re-enters just as ANAIS ducks back into the bedroom. Practicing his "speech":)

FADLEY: I do…I do… Do I?… *(To NONCORT)* Why aren't you in the carriage?

(FADLEY charges past NONCORT and exits.)

NONCORT: That's it, I'm calling the whole thing off!

(Exit NONCORT. EMILE and ANAIS re-emerge, look around cautiously…and they sing.)

> ANAIS & EMILE:
> Alone at last
> Free to look into your eyes
> Love solves everything
> Love heals everyone
> No hat
> No hat
> No hat can come between our love!

(They embrace. Enter UNCLE FEZ. EMILE and ANAIS, startled, separate, as they confront UNCLE FEZ and the musicians)

UNCLE FEZ: A uniform. Are you with the wedding band?

EMILE: Sir! I am an army officer.

UNCLE FEZ: I play a bit of clarinet myself. *(As he shuffles off)* I'll be in the kitchen, comforting a chambermaid. See that we're not disturbed. *(He turns back.)* And incidentally, Miss: shouldn't you be wearing a hat? There is such a thing as common decency.

(UNCLE FEZ exits. ANAIS and EMILE look at one another in alarm, then duck into the bedroom and close the door.)

(A little transition music)

END OF ACT ONE

ACT TWO

Scene One

(A hat shop, modest in size and sparsely stocked, as it has only recently opened. Its proprietor, CLARA, is in conversation with an unsatisfactory employee, TARDIVEAU, at present, off)

CLARA: I ask you to be on time, Mister Tardiveau. I ask you to come here to my hat shop six days a week, work the counter and receive a fair wage. Is that too complicated?

(Enter TARDIVEAU, flustered)

TARDIVEAU: No, ma'am.

CLARA: Sundays you have off. Sundays you can be late for anything you like.

TARDIVEAU: Yes, ma'am.

CLARA: I know you had some problems in the past—

TARDIVEAU: Nerves. A nervous condition.

CLARA: You told me it wouldn't interfere with your duties.

TARDIVEAU: It won't. My doctor assured me that I am making steady progress. Everything is under control.

CLARA: Good.

TARDIVEAU: The people who are following me are not there.

CLARA: What people?

TARDIVEAU: The people I imagine. That's why I was late. I had to take the long way 'round to avoid them.

CLARA: But you said they're not there.

TARDIVEAU: They're not. But they don't know that.

CLARA: Look, Mister Tardiveau—

TARDIVEAU: I'm perfectly fine. I work in a hat shop and no one is following me and talking gibberish and trying to upset me. And my goal is the auxiliary police force.

CLARA: What?

TARDIVEAU: You have to start on the auxiliary force.

CLARA: You want to be a policeman?

(TARDIVEAU *nods.*)

CLARA: Why?

TARDIVEAU: If anyone is following me…I can arrest them.

CLARA: Can we get back to work now?

TARDIVEAU: Yes, ma'am.

CLARA: Go try on that graduation robe that came in. I have an order for two dozen mortarboards and I need a model. Go on.

(TARDIVEAU *exits, after making certain that no one is following him… Music…*)

CLARA: Six months ago I started my own business…

And it's all been a breeze
except for maybe customers
and employees.
(*She feels the urge to sing, succumbs to it*)

A girl can make it on her own
Sure, I'm alone
But I'm not lonely

A girl can finally succeed
She has no need
Of one man only

Sure I took a few false steps
But no regrets
This girl's no phony

I have my dreams, I have my goal
I have my heart, I have my soul

When I'm down I have my song.
Can that be wrong?
If so then show me

I won't play the little wife.
The perfect life?
That's pure baloney!

I know what this heart is for
I don't have to marry
The first loser who walks in the door.

(Enter FADLEY, *breathless, in a hurry.)*

FADLEY: I need a hat—large, ugly, Italian straw with fake fruit—

*(*CLARA *turns and sees him; they both freeze.)*

CLARA: You.

FADLEY: Clara.

CLARA: The disappearing boyfriend.

FADLEY: No, it's not like that at all—

CLARA: You left me standing outside that restaurant in the rain.

FADLEY: I gave you money for a cab.

CLARA: Money? You handed me a laundry receipt!

FADLEY: *(Caught in the act)* I thought it was a dollar bill—

CLARA: You told me to wait while you went to get an umbrella. Here you are, six months later—and no umbrella!

FADLEY: Clara, darling, you're exaggerating. It's only five and a half months. And as for the umbrella…let me go see if I can find one.

CLARA: Oh no you don't. You're lucky I don't call a cop.

FADLEY: The police?

CLARA: Breach of promise. We were supposed to discuss marriage, do you remember that?

FADLEY: I do. Remember, I mean.

CLARA: Ha! How am I supposed to trust you now?

FADLEY: All right. I admit it. A beautiful, attractive girl, the thought of settling down. I panicked. Can you forgive me, Clara?

CLARA: Oh, Winslow. We were so special together.

FADLEY: Were we? We were, yes! Clara, listen. I have this wedding—

CLARA: You're getting married!?

FADLEY: No! A distant cousin, hardly know her. She needs a hat. Just like this, but intact.

CLARA: We only have it in straw.

FADLEY: I'll take it.

CLARA: On one condition. Dinner and a show tonight.

FADLEY: Tonight?

CLARA: Go find your own hat.

FADLEY: Tonight is perfect. No plans. Eight o'clock?

CLARA: Come back to my office, I'll see what I have in stock.

(Exit CLARA *and* FADLEY. *Enter* NONCORT, HELEN, BOBBY.*)*

NONCORT: That's it, I'm calling the whole thing off!

HELEN: Papa...

NONCORT: Where did he disappear to now?

BOBBY: This doesn't look like a Justice of the Peace's office to me.

HELEN: Papa, I still have the pin stuck.

NONCORT: Walk around and stomp your feet.

*(*HELEN *does so.)*

NONCORT: All right, now listen to me, you two. This is a solemn ceremony in front of a legal judge. I want class and I want dignity. *(He shakes his foot.)*

BOBBY: Landscapers have dignity. Get it? *Dig*-nity?

NONCORT: Do you need to go wait in the carriage? Everyone be sure you have your gloves on.

BOBBY: I think I lost one.

NONCORT: Well, put your hand in your pocket.

*(*BOBBY *puts his gloved hand in his pocket)*

NONCORT: Not that one, you idiot.

*(*BOBBY *corrects his error. Enter* TARDIVEAU, *wearing the graduation robe. He freezes when he sees the others and stifles a cry of distress.)*

(Sung, rather beautifully, in a cappella harmony:)

> NONCORT: Your Honor.
> BOBBY: Your Honor.
> HELEN: Your Honor.

(The men bow, HELEN *curtsies.)*

(A stifled moan from TARDIVEAU*)*

NONCORT: We've been waiting for you, Your Judgeship.

BOBBY: We're from Long Island.

NONCORT: I present, sir: the bride.

BOBBY: I'm his nephew.

HELEN: This is my cousin.

NONCORT: I am the father.

BOBBY: I'm the cousin.

NONCORT: We await your instructions, Your Excellency.

TARDIVEAU: Everything...is under control.

NONCORT: Yes, Your Honor.

BOBBY: Thank you, Your Honor.

TARDIVEAU: I am making steady progress.

NONCORT: Very good, Your Honor.

TARDIVEAU: And you...all of you...are present in my imagination.

HELEN: Thank you, Your Honor.

NONCORT: It is an honor, Your Honor.

TARDIVEAU: Talk gibberish, if you like. Go ahead. It won't disturb me.

NONCORT: We're American, Your Honor.

BOBBY: We speak English.

TARDIVEAU: Fine, fine. Do I look disturbed to you?

NONCORT: No, Your Honor.

TARDIVEAU: I have been fully instructed in what to do about you. I want you to know that.

NONCORT: Yes, Your Honor.

TARDIVEAU: So let me ask you directly: Are you following me?

NONCORT: Yes, Your Honor. Perfectly.

TARDIVEAU: Fine. Now we know.

NONCORT: But we can't go any further until the groom shows up.

TARDIVEAU: Ha.

BOBBY: We saw him come in here.

TARDIVEAU: Let me tell you something: If I turn and close my eyes, really tight, you will be gone, just like that. *(He turns away and shuts his eyes.)*

BOBBY: *(To* NONCORT*)* What does he mean?

HELEN: What does he mean, Papa?

NONCORT: He means... He means human life. That it's over... All of it... In the blink of an eye!

HELEN: Oh Papa!

BOBBY: That's pretty depressing, if you ask me.

TARDIVEAU: *(Opening his eyes, turning back and seeing that they are still there)* So. Worthy opponents. If I leave...you'll follow me, won't you.

NONCORT: Yes, Your Honor.

HELEN: Yes, Your Honor.

TARDIVEAU: So be it. Let the contest begin.

*(*TARDIVEAU *bolts, left. A beat. They look at one another, puzzled.)*

HELEN: Maybe we should have done a church wedding.

NONCORT: Oh, and stick me with the bill? Justice of the Peace is a fraction of the cost.

BOBBY: Where did he go?

NONCORT: Back to his chambers. You heard the judge: follow him.

(They exit, in pursuit of TARDIVEAU. *Enter, right,* FADLEY *and* CLARA*)*

FADLEY: I can't believe it! Damn the luck!

CLARA: The last one in stock. You won't find another one like it in New York.

FADLEY: Who did you sell it to?

CLARA: Society type. A baroness, I think.

FADLEY: I'll buy it back. Or borrow it, or steal it. What's her address?

CLARA: *(Looking in her little card file)* Winslow, who cares about a silly hat, now that we've found each other again?

(Enter running TARDIVEAU, *in robes. He halts, breathless.)*

CLARA: Mister Tardiveau, what in the world…?

TARDIVEAU: *(Not daring to look behind him)* Are they there?

CLARA: This is unacceptable behavior in my hat shop. There is no one following you. Look.

*(*TARDIVEAU *looks. There is no one)*

TARDIVEAU: *(A nervous laugh)* Ha. Imagination plays tricks…

CLARA: Pull yourself together, Tardiveau, for pity's sake.

(Enter running BOBBY. *He halts, breathless.)*

BOBBY: Your Honor!

(Enter running HELEN. *She halts, breathless.)*

HELEN: Your Honor!

(Enter running NONCORT. *He halts, breathless.)*

NONCORT: Your Honor! We follow you to your chambers, sir!

TARDIVEAU: *(Barely holding it together; to* CLARA*)* I may need a few days off.
(To prove his point, he tries a song)

> Life is so unfair
> When the ones who are not there
> Won't go away.

> NONCORT, HELEN, BOBBY:
> We will stay,
> Your Honor, we will stay.

> TARDIVEAU: This torture I insist,
> Must cease and desist.
> So disappear!

> NONCORT, HELEN, BOBBY:
> We are here,
> Your Honor, we are here.

> TARDIVEAU: This sign I must heed.
> Further treatment I may need
> For this ill.

> NONCORT, HELEN, BOBBY:
> As you will,
> Your Honor, as you will!

TARDIVEAU: I will never surrender!

*(*TARDIVEAU *bolts, right, and exits. The others follow:* BOBBY, *then* HELEN, *then* NONCORT, *who pauses just before he leaves.)*

NONCORT: *(To* FADLEY*)* Well, don't just stand there!

*(*NONCORT *exits)*

CLARA: Who *are* those people?

FADLEY: Clara, I need that address *now*. Please? For your boyfriend?

CLARA: *(Finding it)* Here it is. Baroness de Champigny.

(FADLEY reaches for it, CLARA withholds it)

CLARA: Ah! First a little kiss.

(FADLEY obliges; CLARA exaggerates. As they are locked in the kiss, re-enter TARDIVEAU, followed by BOBBY, HELEN and NONCORT, in that order. The three members of the wedding party freeze when they see the groom in a compromising position.)

BOBBY: Oh!

HELEN: Oh!

NONCORT: Oh!

CLARA: *(Letting him go)* I have customers now, darling. Run along.

FADLEY: Right. Good idea. *(He exits quickly.)*

CLARA: How may I serve you?

HELEN: The liar!

BOBBY: The cheat!

NONCORT: That's it, I'm calling the whole thing off!

(Exit HELEN and BOBBY, in pursuit of FADLEY.)

CLARA: May I help you, sir?

NONCORT: Fie, Madam! You shameless Jezebel! I will petition this judge to charge you with violation of the morals laws! *(He exits.)*

TARDIVEAU: *(His eyes closed)* Are they gone?

CLARA: Tardiveau.

TARDIVEAU: Yes, ma'am.

CLARA: You're fired.

TARDIVEAU: *(Relieved)* Oh, thank you, ma'am.

(A little more transition music. Lights)

Scene Two

(The street, somewhere near the hat shop. HELEN, *justifiably furious.* FADLEY *tries valiantly to explain his way out of it)*

FADLEY: Helen. Honey. I'm telling you, that was my cousin. We haven't seen each other since elementary school.

HELEN: That was not a cousin kiss!

FADLEY: She was excited.

HELEN: That's what I'm talking about!

FADLEY: No, for me.

HELEN: Oh!

FADLEY: I mean for us—that we're getting married.

HELEN: Winslow Fadley, are you trying to make a fool out of me?

FADLEY: No. It's all just sort of happening on its own.

HELEN: No more nonsense! We are getting married before anything worse happens, and then *you* are taking me home.

FADLEY: Home, absolutely. But maybe we should wait a few days until the weather improves.

HELEN: There's not a cloud in the sky.

FADLEY: That's just what they said before the Blizzard of 1898.

HELEN: *(A shrill, two-fingered whistle)* Papa!

(Enter NONCORT *and* BOBBY. *They take up positions on either side of* FADLEY*)*

HELEN: He's getting cold feet.

NONCORT: That might be a blessing, Helen.

BOBBY: It *is* a blessing!

HELEN: *(All business)* There's a Justice of the Peace on the next block.

(She snaps her fingers. NONCORT and BOBBY each grab an arm, lift FADLEY, turn, and drag him swiftly upstage.)

FADLEY: Hey! Whoa!

HELEN: *(A sweet smile)* Till death do us part, dear.

(They're gone. Still with a smile)

HELEN: You try to jilt me, and that'll be *your* death. *(She sings, damn it.)*

> He needs me
> But doesn't know it
> He's afraid
> And just can't show it
> He simply cannot see
> The best thing that ever happened to him
> Is me
> Is me
>
> He loves me
> But would deny it
> He might bail
> Just let him try it
> I'm going to make him see
> The best thing that ever happened to him
> Is me
> Is me
>
> I'm his answer, I'm his blessing
> I'm the creamy blue-cheese dressing
> On the salad of his life
> The boring salad of his life
>
> I'm his lighthouse on the shore
> No one will ever love him more!

He needs me
He has to face it
Nagging doubt
Time will erase it
I will force him to see
The best thing that ever happened to him
Is me
It's me!

(The bride now joins her groom upstage for the wedding ceremony. FADLEY is still held firmly in place by NONCORT and BOBBY. A few bars of Here Comes The Bride *and the deed is done…)*

(A kiss from HELEN. Then the wedding party exits, triumphantly—HELEN, anyway, is triumphant—and FADLEY is left alone a moment. He looks stunned.)

FADLEY: I'm married? *(He feels himself all over)* It happened so fast, I wasn't ready!

(Enter FADLEY's domestic, FELIX)

FELIX: Mister Fadley, sir.

FADLEY: Felix, do I look different to you? Older? Boring? Trapped?

FELIX: Now that you mention it, Mister Fadley…

FADLEY: What is it you want?

FELIX: The soldier sent me, sir. He's in a rage. He's breaking the furniture.

FADLEY: Felix, you have my permission to toss that adulterer out on the street.

FELIX: He'd never agree to it, sir. The lady had another fainting spell. He put her to bed and called for the doctor.

FADLEY: There's a woman in my bed!?

FELIX: Without a hat.

FADLEY: Felix. Tell them I found the hat. I'll have it all worked out in a matter of minutes. Go!

(*Exit* FELIX)

FADLEY: This is unacceptable...I've been married for two minutes and I'm already in trouble! (*Gathering himself together. Bravado*) But I am a married man now. With a marriage bed. And privileges... The only thing standing between me and bliss is a stupid hat!
(*The new* FADLEY)

> Now finally I see
> The best thing that ever happened to her
> Is me!
> It's me!
> It's me!

I am going to take back my home!
(*He exits.*)

(*Lights. Transition. Music*)

END OF ACT TWO

ACT THREE

(The elegant residence of the BARONESS DE CHAMPIGNY. *The open double doors, center rear, offer a glimpse of the dining hall. The* BARONESS *is consulting with her friend the* VISCOUNT ACHILLES VON ROMANOV, *Russian émigré, who, truth be told, is a bore and a slacker. He is also a shameless flatterer, but only with those who exceed him in wealth or reputation. He surveys the décor.)*

VISCOUNT: It is prodigious, my dear Baroness. How do you do it? The menu, the décor. Fully and entirely prodigious, that is the word. Unless. Unless we must speak...of "breath-taking".

BARONESS: It's only a dinner party, Viscount. I see no reason to asphyxiate.

VISCOUNT: But no, not dinner party. Dinner event. The Baroness de Champigny, arbiter of taste and style for all New York City. For America itself.

BARONESS: Viscount. What causes a dirigible to be airborne?

VISCOUNT: A dirigible? Why, hot air, Baroness.

BARONESS: Yes. And I believe *you* could flatter the Zeppelin into flight.

VISCOUNT: *(Not quite following that)* Yes. Thank you, Baroness.

BARONESS: *(Surveying the menu)* I wonder now if oysters were the right choice. Oysters have no... What is the word?

VISCOUNT: Shells.

BARONESS: Gravitas.

VISCOUNT: Replace them, Baroness, is my advice.

BARONESS: I shall keep them.

VISCOUNT: Keep them, is my advice. How many guests are we expecting?

BARONESS: Fifty-two.

VISCOUNT: The perfect number, what symmetry. Baroness, I have prodigiously good news for you. I have composed a song for the afternoon's entertainment.

BARONESS: You?

VISCOUNT: For piano and tenor. I shall sing it personally.

BARONESS: Aie!

VISCOUNT: I call it *Shiver of Desire*.

BARONESS: The very thought sends a shiver.

VISCOUNT: Yes, thank you.

BARONESS: I am sorry to disappoint you, Viscount, but I have hired a professional vocalist. Nisnardi.

VISCOUNT: "Nisnardi"?

BARONESS: The famous opera singer, the Nightingale of Bologna.

VISCOUNT: But, but—

BARONESS: He is a rising international star.

VISCOUNT: You know him?

BARONESS: I have never laid eyes upon him. He sang last month for the Countess de Bray. In payment, he asked for a single slipper.

VISCOUNT: A lady's slipper?

BARONESS: A charming gesture.

VISCOUNT: Is that not...perverse?

BARONESS: He is an artist, Viscount. Eccentric, romantic—and Italian.

VISCOUNT: Yes, I see. Prodigious. We can sing together!

BARONESS: Aie. *(Hearing the sound)* I hear a carriage. Nisnardi! He promised to arrive early to verify the acoustics. Greet him for me, Viscount. I shall need my better diamonds.

(BARONESS exits, right. Enter a servant, FARNSWORTH, left)

FARNSWORTH: Sir. A gentleman asks to see the Baroness. He refuses to give his name.

VISCOUNT: Farnsworth, you idiot. You have left the Nightingale of Bologna standing in the hallway! Show him in!

(FARNSWORTH exits quickly. Enter FADLEY, uncertainly, looking around.)

FADLEY: Excuse me, sir... This is impossible to explain, but I am looking for a Baroness.

VISCOUNT: And she, dear sir, is looking for you.

FADLEY: She is?

VISCOUNT: She is honored that you are here. Prodigiously. As am I, sir.

FADLEY: Really?

VISCOUNT: The Viscount von Romanov, at your service.

FADLEY: A viscount!

VISCOUNT: I apologize for the way you were greeted by that idiot servant. He will be fired, rest assured.

FADLEY: Fired?

VISCOUNT: In Russia, he would be shot, *then* fired. I see in your face that proud Roman ancestry. You look so prodigiously Bolognese.

FADLEY: *(Not getting it)* What about my knees?

VISCOUNT: And yet, you speak with almost no accent. Remarkable. Dear sir, I declare to you this: while you are here, I am honor-bound to fulfill your every wish.

FADLEY: Every one?

VISCOUNT: Even…ha, ha…an item from a lady's wardrobe!

FADLEY: Ha, ha. Really?

VISCOUNT: A slipper, perhaps? Ha, ha.

FADLEY: How about a hat?

VISCOUNT: A hat, of course. Prodigious.

FADLEY: That's perfect! You know, Viscount, I think my luck is changing.

VISCOUNT: Tell me this: How do you find the acoustics?

FADLEY: I'm no good at geography. Are they anywhere near the Bahamas?

VISCOUNT: Indeed. You and I, sir: we are confreres.

FADLEY: Is that Italian?

VISCOUNT: Music, we make pure music! The passion, the intensity! The love, sir, if you will permit me.

FADLEY: Permit you to what?

VISCOUNT: *Shiver of Desire.* A little "invention" of mine. Tell me, what do you think?

FADLEY: What do I think?

VISCOUNT: Be frank, sir, as only an Italian master can be.

FADLEY: Well, it sounds a little perverse.

VISCOUNT: You must understand, sir, how deeply, how prodigiously I admire you.

FADLEY: Me?

VISCOUNT: I toss caution to the wind and propose to you, sir...

FADLEY: Propose to me?

VISCOUNT: Sir, yes! This: *(Confidentially)* Duet.

FADLEY: Do what?

VISCOUNT: Duet.

FADLEY: Who?

VISCOUNT: You and I, sir. Here, this day, in this very room.

FADLEY: Whoa, whoa—

VISCOUNT: So. I'm not good enough for you.

FADLEY: It's not that—

VISCOUNT: I, Viscount Achilles von Romanov, am nothing, the dust on your boot.

FADLEY: No, look—

VISCOUNT: I beg you, sir: give me a chance to delight you. That is all I ask. *(He takes off his coat.)*

FADLEY: Hold it right there! I know you society types play by your own rules, but all I want is a hat.

VISCOUNT: You wild eccentric, you! I grant you your wish, sir.

FADLEY: You do?

VISCOUNT: If you will grant me mine.

FADLEY: I can't— I mean, I never—I just don't know if I can *do* that, Viscount!

VISCOUNT: Let me show you, privately, my part.

FADLEY: No, please—!

VISCOUNT: I warn you: it is prodigious.

FADLEY: I really don't care—!

VISCOUNT: Wait here. I go to find my pianist. *(He pronounces it, of course, "penis". He hurries off.)*

FADLEY: What, you can't *find* it!? What kind of a madhouse have I wandered into? I only want a hat, I don't want to be arrested for public lewdness.

(Enter the BARONESS.)

BARONESS: Dear, dear sir! What an honor that you have come.

FADLEY: Are you—?

BARONESS: Baroness Elizabeth Juliette Olivia Hélène de Champigny.

FADLEY: Five names! You *must* be important.

BARONESS: You have met the Viscount?

FADLEY: Yes, ma'am— I mean, Your Baroness-ship. He went off to get his, his—

BARONESS: Not his *Shiver of Desire*?

FADLEY: That's just what he called it. Do you condone that kind of thing?

BARONESS: I try to discourage it, sir. But sometimes there is no holding these old gentlemen back.

FADLEY: That's scary.

BARONESS: It is remarkable, but your accent is almost undetectable. Tell me: how do you find the acoustics?

FADLEY: Turn left at Cuba?

BARONESS: Let us speak, dear sir, of the reason you grace us with your presence.

FADLEY: I was just getting to that. I don't know how to put this, exactly. It sounds sort of strange…

BARONESS: Or "eccentric"?

FADLEY: Eccentric, right. But I want something of yours. If it's a matter of money…

BARONESS: Let us not degrade ourselves with talk of money.

FADLEY: Right. Money: blech! But what I need— To you, it's just an item from your wardrobe, but to me, it's the key to my whole future.

BARONESS: Dear sir! I know precisely what you desire.

FADLEY: You do?

BARONESS: Yes! And it shall be yours.

FADLEY: Gosh, that's great news! Baroness, you are one of the least snobby upper-class people I have ever met.

BARONESS: Sir, I am but a baroness. You are an artist.

FADLEY: Me?

BARONESS: An internationally acclaimed star of the opera.

FADLEY: Me??

BARONESS: The great Rodolpho Nisnardi, the Nightingale of Bologna! It is an honor, sir, to grant your every request. Will you follow me? *(She exits.)*

FADLEY: Whoa… I'm an Italian opera star?
(And now what else? A song. But with an appropriately operatic flair, of course)

> But I'll have the hat
> What's wrong with that?
> I say "grazie" and go home.

Clear out those squatters,
And we're alone
Helen and I,
Alone at last.
And our bed,
Our glorious nuptial
Marriage bed—!

Consummazione! Ecstasio!

It's perfect!
What could go wrong?
What could go wrong?
What could possibly go wrong?

(He exits.)

(Calling, off)

NONCORT: *(Off)* Son-in-law!

HELEN: *(Off)* Honey?

(Enter NONCORT with plant, HELEN, BOBBY.)

NONCORT: Your new husband keeps disappearing, Helen, that's not a good sign. What kind of a restaurant *is* this?

BOBBY: A snobby one.

HELEN: Oh, Papa. Oysters!

(She enters the dining hall, transfixed)

NONCORT: Helen, don't overdo it, we barely got you into that wedding dress. *(To BOBBY)* Nobody told me about a reception with oysters. Where's the maitre d'? When we get to seventy-five dollars, I want this party shut down.

BOBBY: *(Looking in the dining hall)* Hey, Uncle Karl. Champagne! *(He exits into the dining hall.)*

NONCORT: Champagne!? What do I look like, the King of England?

(Exit NONCORT *into the dining hall. Enter the* BARONESS, *right, followed by* FADLEY*)*

BARONESS: Ah, you Italian artists! My servant will return momentarily with your prize.

FADLEY: Good. And then I'll have to say ciao, Baroness.

BARONESS: But not before you sing! Fifty-two of my wealthiest friends will arrive shortly to attend your concert.

FADLEY: My concert, of course, what was I thinking?

BARONESS: And what will you sing?

FADLEY: Well, Baroness, that's going to be sort of a surprise.

(Rapidly here, as she advances on him and he retreats:)

BARONESS: I have a request: Leoncavallo.

FADLEY: I could lay on the cavallo, but I'm not tired, thanks.

BARONESS: Would you do Puccini for me?

FADLEY: For you, I'd *walk* the pooch-eeny.

BARONESS: Or perhaps *Orpheo and Eurydice.*

FADLEY: I'm a what?

BARONESS: *Nessun Dorma*?

FADLEY: Nice and short, too.

BARONESS: Or *Manon Lescaut.*

FADLEY: The "let's go" part I like.

BARONESS: *(A flash of anger)* Such relentlessly eccentric humor!

(Enter FARNSWORTH, *carrying a satin pillow draped with a silk cloth)*

Ah. Your request, sir.

FADLEY: At last! If you knew the problems this solves, Baroness. *(He removes the cloth to find a woman's slipper.)* What the hell is this!?

BARONESS: A slipper from my personal wardrobe.

FADLEY: *(Losing it)* What do I want with a slipper!?

BARONESS: Sir!

FADLEY: I want a hat! The one you bought last week!

BARONESS: How do you know about that?

FADLEY: Italian artists are very attached to their hats. In fact… Without a hat, I can't sing. I can't breathe!

BARONESS: Signor Nisnardi!

FADLEY: *(Choking)* No hat…no concert!

BARONESS: This is more eccentric than I can tolerate! *(To the* SERVANT*)* Quickly! My wardrobe!

(Exit the BARONESS *and the* SERVANT, *hurriedly)*

FADLEY: Why do I have this sense of doom?

(The dining hall door bursts open. NONCORT, HELEN, BOBBY *appear, singing, all of them at least slightly drunk on champagne. They sing, or rather butcher, a couple of lines to* Yankee Doodle Dandy*)*

NONCORT, BOBBY, HELEN:
I'm a Yankee Doodle Dandy,
Yankee Doodle do or die!...

HELEN: Oh! Those oysters were so good! I must've ate three dozen.

FADLEY: What are you doing!?

BOBBY: Great spot for a reception, Fadley. But you're still a snob.

NONCORT: *(An announcement)* Today is my baby daughter's wedding day. Forget the seventy-five dollar shut-off. Make it eight-five!

(Cheers and whooping)

FADLEY: Keep it down!

NONCORT: *(A formal speech)* Friends and loved ones. The time has come for some brief remarks.

FADLEY: *(Herding everyone back into the dining hall)* Get back in there! They're bringing more champagne!

(FADLEY gets them all in, closes the doors just as the BARONESS enters, followed by FARNSWORTH, carrying a hat box)

BARONESS: I hope *this* will satisfy you.

FADLEY: *(Reaching for the hat box)* Baroness! You're an angel.

BARONESS: Not so swiftly, sir. Sing.

FADLEY: What, here?

BARONESS: A small aria.

FADLEY: It's a pretty big area, if you have to sing in it. I need my hat first.

BARONESS: To paraphrase you, sir: No concert, no hat.

(Suddenly the dining hall door opens and NONCORT appears, champagne glass in hand, napkin tucked into his collar. He is in mid-speech)

NONCORT: "A man's life...is like a shrub."

BARONESS: Who, pray, is this?

FADLEY: This is— He's my— He's accompanying me.

BARONESS: Ah! Your pianist. *(Same pronunciation, of course)*

(Double-take: NONCORT and FADLEY both look at their private parts)

NONCORT: You must be the hostess.

BARONESS: I beg your pardon, sir.

NONCORT: Pardon granted, lady, but we ran out of oysters in here, so get on the stick.

BARONESS: My oysters! Farnsworth!

(The BARONESS swoons, slumps in a chair. FARNSWORTH hands the hat box to FADLEY, hurries to this employer's rescue. As he fans her, FADLEY rips open the box and pulls out...the wrong hat.)

FADLEY: At last, at last... No! It's the wrong hat! Italian straw, big, ugly, with fake fruit!

FARNSWORTH: I know that one. The Baroness gave it to her niece for her birthday.

FADLEY: Name!

FARNSWORTH: Farnsworth, Chester L.

FADLEY: The niece, you idiot!

FARNSWORTH: Beauperthuis. *(Pronounced "Bo-per-twee")*

FADLEY: Bo-per what?

FARNSWORTH: It's French.

FADLEY: That can't be helped. Address!

FARNSWORTH: Central Park West at 65th.

(As FADLEY prepares to make a hasty exit, left, enter the VISCOUNT, walking FADLEY back into the room.)

VISCOUNT: Maestro!

FADLEY: Oh no.

VISCOUNT: My *Shiver of Desire*!

NONCORT: Say, what kind of a restaurant *is* this, anyway?

VISCOUNT: I have looked everywhere, sir, but I cannot locate my—

FADLEY: Don't say it! Even a Vaudeville farce can't get away with the same bad pun forever.

(The dining hall doors open. HELEN *and* BOBBY *burst into the salon with shouts and laughter.* HELEN *does the traditional if drunken toss of the bouquet... The* BARONESS, *revived now, has had enough)*

BARONESS: Halt! Halt, I say! Farnsworth, bar the exit.

*(*FARNSWORTH *physically blocks the exit.)*

BARONESS: Now, sir. Sing.

FADLEY: Without my music?

BARONESS: Sing a cappella.

FADLEY: I don't know anything by Cappella.

BARONESS: Sing!

FADLEY: Baroness, do you speak Italian?

BARONESS: Not a word.

FADLEY: Good.
(Operatically)

> *Arrivederci*
> Ze hat I search-ay...
> *O mi amore*
> Where's my fedor-ay?

(Before he can disgrace himself further, enter a man, left, dressed theatrically)

NISNARDI: *(With accent) Buon giorno,* my admirers, I am come! Rodolpho Nisnardi, the Nightingale of Bologna! *(He bows)*

(All eyes to FADLEY. *A beat)*

FADLEY: It all started when my horse ate this hat...
(He begins edging toward the exit. His only hope now: song)

> Those who have a passion
> For items of high fashion
> Often find

> ALL THE OTHERS: They often find

FADLEY: They're in a bind

OTHERS: An awful bind

FADLEY: It's that tragic obsession
A hunger for possession
Of a hat

OTHERS: A simple hat
No more than that

FADLEY: *(Spoken)* It's not simple, believe me.

OTHERS: How will his extrication
From this foul impersonation
Finally end?

BARONESS: Before I send

OTHERS: Before she sends

BARONESS: For the police.

FADLEY: I tell you how.

OTHERS: How?

FADLEY: I say it now.

OTHERS: Now?

FADLEY: I say *ciao*!

OTHERS: He says *ciao*! He says *ciao*!
He says *Ciao! Ciao! Ciao!*
He says *ciao*! He says *ciao*!

NISNARDI: I am come!

OTHERS: He is come!

NISNARDI: I am come!

OTHERS: He is come!

(FADLEY *attempts to escape, but he is prevented from exiting by various singing characters... The song and the scene build to an operatic end as* FADLEY *manages at last to exit, with the real* NISNARDI *downstage center, out-singing everyone, as only an Italian master can do.)*

NISNARDI: I say *ciao!*

OTHERS: He says *ciao!*
He says *ciao!*
He says *ciao! Ciao! Ciao!*

(Etc)

(Lights. Relief)

END OF ACT THREE

INTERMISSION

ACT FOUR

(The apartment of MR NAPOLEON BEAUPERTHUIS, *a rather humorless, self-important type who is presently in a very foul temper. He is dressed—or rather, semi-dressed—in towels. He is seated on a wooden chair, his feet in a tub of water. He is surrounded by a curtain, now open, on a circular ring, rather like a shower stall. The footbath was once a popular remedy against headaches, and he is experiencing a splitting one, due in part to the prolonged and unexplained absence of his young wife... He is speaking, apparently, to someone not present.)*

BEAUPERTHUIS: What do I look like to you? Some kind of laughing stock? I did not rise up to where I am today by being a laughing stock, believe you me. I started with nothing. I had *less* than nothing. I was so hungry one winter, I ate tree bark. Flowering magnolia. It has to be boiled for hours. I turned myself into New York City's leading wholesaler of bathroom fixtures in a single generation—on tree bark. So don't try to make a laughing stock out of Napoleon P Beauperthuis, because you will fail.

(Enter VIRGINIA, *with a tea kettle.)*

VIRGINIA: More, sir?

BEAUPERTHUIS: Go on.

*(*VIRGINIA *pours a little hot water into* BEAUPERTHUIS's *footbath.)*

BEAUPERTHUIS: Ow! Damn it!

VIRGINIA: You said make it hot.

BEAUPERTHUIS: But not scalding!

VIRGINIA: Sorry.

BEAUPERTHUIS: Leave it there! *(The kettle)* A footbath requires tepid water, not molten lava!

VIRGINIA: How is your headache now, Mister B?

BEAUPERTHUIS: It's worse!

VIRGINIA: I didn't know you could cure a headache by soaking your feet.

BEAUPERTHUIS: You're a maid, what do you know about medical science? *(A beat)* Eight-fifty-three A M, she leaves the apartment. "I'm going to shop for a pair of English leather gloves, dear." Here it is, 9:02 P M. Don't try to tell me it takes twelve hours and nine minutes to buy a pair of English leather gloves—unless you sail to England!

VIRGINIA: Yes, Mister B.

(She starts to leave)

BEAUPERTHUIS: Are you sure you tried everyone?

VIRGINIA: Yes, Mister B. No one's seen her.

BEAUPERTHUIS: What about her favorite dress shops?

VIRGINIA: It would take a week.

BEAUPERTHUIS: Well, then get started!

(VIRGINIA exits.)

BEAUPERTHUIS: If there's another man: bloodshed.
(His anger leads him to song.)

>   I hereby declare it,
>   By the honorable name
>   Of Beauperthuis!

This could end disastrously.

A marital scandal?
My business cannot handle
Such publicity.

"There goes that sorry cuckold
Beauperthuis!"

Bathroom fixtures, I sell to the elites.
But with a wife who cheats?
They'll snub me in the streets.

"There goes that sorry cuckold
Beauperthuis!"
"We'll not buy commodes
From such as he!
"Fie, fie that sorry cuckold
Beauperthuis!"

(A knock on the door)

BEAUPERTHUIS: Well, it's about time. It's open! I hope you brought a plausible explanation with you, "dear".

(Enter FADLEY, out of breath.)

FADLEY: It's you. Tell me it's you.

BEAUPERTHUIS: What is the meaning of this, sir? What are you doing in my apartment?

FADLEY: I don't know you, but I know you. Beauperthuis, right?

BEAUPERTHUIS: Who are you!?

FADLEY: There's no time to explain—even if I could. I think the police are after me.

BEAUPERTHUIS: Oh, a robbery, is it? Strip me of my valuables in my own home!

FADLEY: You're taking a footbath? What is it, a headache? *(He takes the tea kettle.)*

BEAUPERTHUIS: That is none of your business!

FADLEY: You want to keep it tepid. *(He pours some water)*

BEAUPERTHUIS: Owww! Assassin!

FADLEY: I am here to talk about a hat.

BEAUPERTHUIS: So. An escaped lunatic. Your case is hopeless, sir, they will track you down.

FADLEY: My name is Winslow C Fadley, residing at 219 East 83rd, I have just gotten married and I am interested in one thing only: your wife.

BEAUPERTHUIS: My wife! So it's you, you home-wrecker! Where is she?

FADLEY: I have no idea, I've never laid eyes on her. I am here, sir, for an item of clothing from her wardrobe and I'm not leaving without it.

BEAUPERTHUIS: You want my wife's clothes? On your wedding day? What is happening to the moral fabric of this city?

FADLEY: Where is she?

BEAUPERTHUIS: She is not here.

FADLEY: At nine o'clock at night? *(He brandishes the tea kettle.)* You let your wife run around the city at all hours? *(He pours.)*

BEAUPERTHUIS: Aie!!

FADLEY: Where's her bedroom?

BEAUPERTHUIS: You get out of my apartment!

(FADLEY pours again.)

BEAUPERTHUIS: Aie!! In there!

FADLEY: I'm warning you, sir… *(He snatches the towel from BEAUPERTHUIS's shoulders.)* I am a desperate man.

(FADLEY snatches the towel from BEAUPERTHUIS's waist, leaving him naked.)

BEAUPERTHUIS: Aie!!

FADLEY: Don't move.

(FADLEY *pulls the curtain, mercifully hiding*
BEAUPERTHUIS, *then exits to the bedroom, right.)*

BEAUPERTHUIS: *(His head appears between the curtains)*
Trapped by a lunatic transvestite in my own home!

(He hears someone coming, left)

BEAUPERTHUIS: Another one!

(BEAUPERTHUIS *hides behind the curtain. Enter* NONCORT.*)*

NONCORT: Son-in-law? *(He spies a pair of slippers outside
the curtain, apparently belonging to* BEAUPERTHUIS.*)*
Slippers! Oh, thank God. I can walk again.

(As NONCORT *changes his shoes, enter* HELEN, BOBBY*)*

HELEN: Papa? Where are we?

NONCORT: The honeymoon suite, evidently. *(Speaking
to the curtain)* This hotel better be an improvement over
that restaurant, Fadley. Are you ready? *(He reaches for
the curtain.)*

BEAUPERTHUIS: *(From within)* Don't!

NONCORT: He's changing into his night clothes.

HELEN: Papa. Do I have to—? How do I, when do I,
where do I, what do I *do*??

NONCORT: My child.

HELEN: *(Angry)* You were supposed to explain this
part, remember?

BOBBY: Helen, let's go back downstairs.

NONCORT: Bobby, no. The sacred moment of conjugal
union is upon her. *(Taking a proper patriarchal stance)*
The time has come for some words of paternal wisdom.
Son-in-law, don your chamber robe and take your
lawful place at your bride's right hand.

HELEN: No, Papa, please!

NONCORT: Oh all right, then. Listen to my every word, Fadley. This is for your edification, too. Bobby: my myrtle.

(BOBBY *hands him the plant.*)

NONCORT: Kneel, my children.

(HELEN *and* BOBBY *kneel.*)

NONCORT: In every father's life comes the day when he must separate himself forever from the precious little girl he once cradled in his arms.

BOBBY: Do you think they have a toilet on this floor?

NONCORT: Can't you keep your mouth shut until I'm through with this?

BOBBY: I was just asking.

NONCORT: Go pee in the alley if you have to! ...Now I forgot where I was. What was I saying?

HELEN: "Go pee in the alley if you have to."

NONCORT: I remember now... This fragile little flower... Let its precious leaves remind you that you have a father who loves you... And one day, you will make him a grandfather... And I will plant another little tree, just like this...

HELEN: Oh, Papa!

NONCORT: Fadley? Do you have nothing to say at this moment of supreme emotion?

BOBBY: He probably fell asleep in there.

NONCORT: What? During my speech? Fadley!

(NONCORT *pulls back the curtain to reveal a naked* BEAUPERTHUIS, *covering his private parts and looking furious, perhaps psychopathic.* HELEN *screams.* NONCORT *pulls the curtain shut.*)

HELEN: Papa, I never saw him without his clothes on! He looks completely different!

NONCORT: *(Stupefied)* My child—

HELEN: I can't go through with it! I want a divorce.

BOBBY: Helen, let's go down to the front desk.

HELEN: I want a separate room—with a lock!

(HELEN and BOBBY exit, left)

NONCORT: I don't understand…

(Shaken, NONCORT goes to the curtain…gets up the courage to take one last peek…then closes it quickly… A song might help.)

> NONCORT: I only wanted happiness,
> That's all I'm asking for.
> Preserve a little innocence,
> The daughter I adore.
>
> Is this the world
> I gave my little girl?
>
> A world so cruel and cold
> To a father growing old,
> His high hopes fall to earth,
> His dreams of little worth,
> His expectation shrinks.
> Is this the world?
> If so…it stinks!
> That's what this papa thinks:
> It stinks!

(NONCORT exits, shakily, left. Enter FADLEY, right)

FADLEY: It's not here! I've emptied every closet and dumped out every drawer and it's gone! Here.

(FADLEY opens the curtain and tosses BEAUPERTHUIS his two towels, which he hastily puts on.)

FADLEY: I've spent my wedding day running from one side of Manhattan to the other.

BEAUPERTHUIS: Before I have you arrested, you scoundrel, I demand to know what this is all about!

FADLEY: This is about a tragedy, Mister Beauperthuis. A hat, eaten by a horse. A woman, parading around the woods with a soldier. The two of them, refusing to leave my townhouse.

BEAUPERTHUIS: Why don't you just kick them out?

FADLEY: Because there's a husband, that's why!

BEAUPERTHUIS: Another unfaithful wife!

FADLEY: Another idiot husband who can't keep track of his own wife.

BEAUPERTHUIS: Alas.

FADLEY: And he's violent. When he finds her, he'll do something horrible and bloody.

BEAUPERTHUIS: And who can blame him?

FADLEY: But not in my townhouse! Look at this. (*The sample, from his pocket*) It was hers. Italian straw, with fake fruit. Can I find a replacement anywhere in the whole city?

BEAUPERTHUIS: Italian straw… In the woods, you say? With a soldier?

FADLEY: Can you believe it?

BEAUPERTHUIS: (*Darkly*) Oh, I believe it. Wait here.

(*Exit* BEAUPERTHUIS, *right.* FADLEY, *at a loss for words, is not, alas, at a loss for song*)

> FADLEY: It seemed a simple goal this morning:
> A lady's hat. Then without warning
> My life collapsed.
> And now somewhere amid the rubble
> I find not solace but more trouble.

Is it my task
To save a hatless woman's... honor
Before revenge he takes upon her?
I have to ask
Where
Oh where did I go wrong?

(HELEN *appears, apart, to join* FADLEY *in a duet of confused lovers.*)

HELEN: I wanted strong
I wanted brave
A sad lost soul that I can save

FADLEY: I wanted love
I wanted life
Loving arms of a loving wife

HELEN: I wanted faith
I wanted joy
The chance to give him a little boy

FADLEY & HELEN:
I want devotion
Pure emotion
The notion that in sum
Two lives can be as one
Two empty lives fulfilled as one
Two broken lives renewed as one
As one

FADLEY: I wanted kind
I wanted true
Show what I meant when I said I do

HELEN: I wanted safe
I wanted sound
Arms to lift me up when I fall down

FADLEY & HELEN:
I need safe haven
Take this stray in

I'm praying this is right
Just hold me through the night
Two empty lives fulfilled as one
Two broken lives renewed as one
As one

I wanted hearth
I wanted home
A place I never have to be alone
Never alone

(HELEN *withdraws.* VIRGINIA *has entered at the end of this musical lament. She stares at* FADLEY, *puzzled.*)

VIRGINIA: Mister Fadley?

FADLEY: You. What are you doing here?

VIRGINIA: I work here.

FADLEY: Didn't I fire you twelve hours ago?

VIRGINIA: Ssh! You want to get me fired twice in one day? Why are you standing in Mister B's apartment singing to yourself?

(Enter BEAUPERTHUIS, *hastily dressed, except for shoes. He puts on the ones that* NONCORT *exchanged for the slippers)*

VIRGINIA: No luck, Mister B. No one's seen her.

BEAUPERTHUIS: Never mind, Virginia. I know where she is now.

VIRGINIA: Now, Mister B. Take a deep breath.

BEAUPERTHUIS: What I plan to take is revenge.

(BEAUPERTHUIS *withdraws a handgun from his coat pocket.* VIRGINIA *and* FADLEY *embrace in terror. To* FADLEY)

BEAUPERTHUIS: You. Take me to my wife.

FADLEY: Your wife?

BEAUPERTHUIS: The hat was what tipped me off. It was a present from her aunt.

FADLEY: Right, of course, the Baroness—

(The light goes on: PING!)

Whoa, whoa, whoa! You're saying the woman in my townhouse is your *wife*?

BEAUPERTHUIS: *(Darkly)* Without a hat.

FADLEY: Hold it, hold it, time out!

(FADLEY takes a step downstage. To the audience, as he works it out, with the help of some dramatic musical underscoring…)

FADLEY: His wife is the niece with the hat… *(Music!)* Which she hung on a tree branch while she and that soldier… *(Music!)* So the hat that I have been chasing my entire wedding day… *(Music!)* Is the same hat that my horse ate at nine o'clock this morning! *(Music!)* It's horse manure now!! *(Music!)* Oh that is *so* cruel!

BEAUPERTHUIS: Enough babbling! Your place, 219 East 83rd. Let's go.

FADLEY: There's been a major mistake here, Mister Beauperthuis.

BEAUPERTHUIS: And I am about to correct it.

FADLEY: But I just moved into the neighborhood— violence will make a bad impression.

BEAUPERTHUIS: March!

(Exit FADLEY, followed by BEAUPERTHUIS. Dramatic accompaniment from the musicians as VIRGINIA, horrified and at a loss what to do, takes a panicked step right, a panicked step left…then comes to halt, center)

VIRGINIA: The thing of it is… it was such an ugly hat anyway. *(She exits cheerfully.)*

(Lights. Music)

END OF ACT FOUR

ACT FIVE

(*Night. A streetlamp lights the corner outside* FADLEY's *townhouse, upstage center: a step or two leading to a door, an ornamental shrub on either side of the steps. Enter* TARDIVEAU, *the former hat shop clerk, on patrol in his brand new job as an auxiliary policeman. He is doing his best not to show any overt signs of anxiety… He walks along, twirling his baton… stops. Waits a beat, then turns quickly to look behind him. A sigh of relief)*

TARDIVEAU: No one there… Tardiveau, the sergeant said to me, auxiliary policeman is not just a low-paying, thankless job. It's a sacred trust. Your assignment: night patrol, East 60th to East 90th. Walk the streets, be a symbol of justice. Here I am, East 83rd already and not a speck of trouble. (*He looks behind him again. He is happy enough to sing.*)

And I'm alone!
Alone at last,
With no one not there following me.

They're gone!

Gone forever, I declare,
Are the ones who are not there!

I'm free!

A pillar of authority.
Scared of me? You'd better be!

(An heroic stance)
Just look!

A lowly hat shop clerk
You might dare to follow.
An auxiliary policeman
You'd be scared to follow!
Unprepared to follow!
Brain-impaired to follow!

Now I see my life unfold.
My story can be told.
The film rights will be sold!
A Broadway show!
"The Adventures of…
Officer…" No.
"Lieutenant…" No.
"Commissioner…" No. Just…
"Tardiveau!!"

NONCORT: *(Calling, off)* Officer!

TARDIVEAU: What's this? A cry for help.

(TARDIVEAU faces left, peering into the darkness. Enter, from the right, NONCORT, HELEN, BOBBY. They halt. TARDIVEAU senses someone behind him. He does a slow turn…sees them…turns back.)

TARDIVEAU: They're back.

NONCORT: Officer! We are confused by darkness. Direct us to 83rd street, sir. We have a woman suffering from a breach of promise.

TARDIVEAU: O! Pitiless creatures. You may follow me… but you will never defeat me!

(He exits, rapidly, left)

NONCORT: You heard the officer—follow him.

HELEN: Papa, I refuse to go another step.

BOBBY: Why did you send the carriages away, uncle?

NONCORT: Nine dollars and fifty cents an hour? We can walk—now that I've solved my footwear problem.

HELEN: I need to sit down.

NONCORT: Not on the street in a $28 dress.

BOBBY: Uncle, I see a street sign. *This* is 83rd Street.

NONCORT: Luck, at last. Now we retrieve our wedding gifts. I can probably get cash for most of them.

(Enter FELIX, FADLEY'*s servant. He sees* NONCORT *and company)*

FELIX: Uh-oh. *(He turns to leave.)*

NONCORT: Halt, knave! Where is your master's townhouse?

FELIX: You're standing in front of it, sir.

NONCORT: Go in and bring out the wedding gifts.

FELIX: I can't do that, Mister Noncort, sir.

NONCORT: And why not, you rogue?

FELIX: The woman without the hat is lying on the bed.

NONCORT: What!?

HELEN: A woman!

BOBBY: On his bed!

NONCORT: Without a hat!

FELIX: Oh, it's not like you think. I can explain everything. You see…

(They all glare at FELIX, *expectantly. A beat, as he realizes the hopelessness of it)*

FELIX: Forget it.

NONCORT: The gifts! Before I have you arrested as an accomplice to adultery!

*(*FELIX *exits into the townhouse, center.)*

HELEN: Papa? After what I've seen of it...this whole marriage thing is horse manure.

NONCORT: Helen!

BOBBY: She's right, you know.

NONCORT: Who asked for your opinion?

BOBBY: We never should have left our plants and shrubs. *(He goes suddenly, dramatically on bended knee before* HELEN.*)* Helen. I have the brain of a landscaper, but the heart of a lion. I solemnly ask for your hand in divorce.

NONCORT: Have you lost your mind?

(Re-enter FELIX, *with multiple boxes, including the large one that dear* UNCLE FEZ *brought with him way back in* ACT ONE.*)*

FELIX: I think I got them all.

NONCORT: Careful! Some of those might be expensive china.

FELIX: *(Looking offstage)* Uh-oh. *(He exits into the townhouse.)*

(Enter right, running, FADLEY.*)*

FADLEY: I think I lost him, but he has my address. He'll be here any minute—murder, mayhem, bloodshed! *(A beat, as he focuses)* What are you doing with the wedding presents?

NONCORT: Oh!

FADLEY: Bobby?

BOBBY: *(Disgust)* Oh.

FADLEY: Helen, honey?

HELEN: *(Exasperation)* Oh!

NONCORT: I am calling the whole thing off—and bringing criminal charges!

FADLEY: There's no time for that now. We have to help the woman without the hat escape.

HELEN: Oh!

BOBBY: Oh!

NONCORT: Oh... So you admit it! Noncorts: seize your legally owned items and turn your backs on this bigamist forever!

(*They begin to grab all the packages.*)

FADLEY: No, wait. Helen—I can explain everything! Put that down!

(*A tug-of-war with* NONCORT *over the large package that* UNCLE FEZ *brought*)

NONCORT: Let go, you Mormon!

FADLEY: You don't understand!

(*Enter, from the townhouse,* UNCLE FEZ. *Everyone freezes.*)

UNCLE FEZ: Ah, the wedding party at last! I overslept. Have I missed anything?

(*Everyone back to the packages*)

NONCORT: Unhand my gift, you degenerate!

(*In the struggle, the top of the package comes off and out falls...a lady's Italian straw hat with fake fruit*)

UNCLE FEZ: Hey, hey, careful there. That came all the way from Italy.

(UNCLE FEZ *picks it up.* FADLEY *screams.*)

Well, if you don't like it, I can take it back. The damn thing cost me sixty dollars.

NONCORT: (*Impressed*) Sixty dollars?

FADLEY: (*Grabbing it from* UNCLE FEZ) Italian. Straw. With fake fruit!

UNCLE FEZ: *(Grabbing it back)* No, no, it's Italian straw with fake fruit. Sometimes I wonder about you, Winslow.

FADLEY: *(Grabbing it back)* The hat! We're saved! *(His joy conspiring with overexcited nerves, he erupts in song)*

> Gloria!
> Gloria!
> Oh heaven-sent euphoria!
> This crown at last restore-ia!
> Gloria!

ALL: Gloria!
> Gloria!
> Your conduct we deplore-ia
> Divorce we have in store-ia
> Gloria!

FADLEY: My hopes, they all were dead here,
> Then this Holy Grail of headgear
> I did find
> And just in time

ALL: He's lost his mind!

> Such reckless haberdashery
> We knew would end disastrously,
> And we were right!

FADLEY: Oh hat of light!
> Oh wondrous sight!

ALL & FADLEY:
> Gloria!
> Gloria!
> Magnificent sartoria!
> Tiara of Victoria!
> Gloria!

UNCLE FEZ: I think I'll go back upstairs and have a drink.

(Exit UNCLE FEZ *into the townhouse, center.* FADLEY *stuffs the hat back into the hatbox.)*

FADLEY: *(Joyous)* This solves everything, don't you see? I give her the hat, she gives me back my townhouse and we're all normal again!

BOBBY: I got my doubts.

*(*FADLEY *exits into the townhouse, sans hatbox, followed by* FELIX.)*

NONCORT: My children—quickly—the wedding gifts. The sixty dollar hat, too. Then back to Long Island!

(They gather up the packages. NONCORT *swiftly removes the hat, leaving the hatbox. Re-enter auxiliary policeman* TARDIVEAU *hurriedly, out of breath, glancing behind him. He halts before the assembled group.)*

TARDIVEAU: All right, freeze! Nobody move.

(They freeze. TARDIVEAU *tentatively approaches* NONCORT, *reaches out, touches him.)*

TARDIVEAU: You're real. You exist. Do you know what this means? I am cured!

NONCORT: Officer, we don't follow you.

TARDIVEAU: Oh, yes you do! And you're under arrest for it!

HELEN: Arrest!

TARDIVEAU: And for burglary, too!

BOBBY: But officer, there's been some kind of mistake!

TARDIVEAU: Tell it to the sergeant. March! And bring the evidence with you.

(They all exit, right, with packages—except for the now-empty hat box. Enter from the townhouse FADLEY, ANAIS, EMILE.)*

FADLEY: Out, out! And hurry—your husband will be here any second.

ANAIS: You betrayed me, sir!

FADLEY: Lady, just put your hat on and get out of here. *(Reaching in the hat box)* If you knew what it took to get this thing... Ahgh! It's gone!

ANAIS: Emile!

EMILE: Enough of your cruel jokes, sir!

(Preparing to fight, EMILE places his officer's coat around ANAIS's shoulders, hands her his hat.)

FADLEY: This whole day has been a cruel joke. And you owe me for six chairs and an end table!

EMILE: Where is that hat!?

FADLEY: *(Noticing now that they're gone)* Where is my wife? Where are the wedding gifts?

NONCORT: *(Calling, from a distance, off)* Son-in-law! Help us!

FADLEY: *(Looking off, right)* My wedding is being arrested. That old miser—he has the hat!

EMILE: I'll go. I outrank an auxiliary policeman. *(He hurries off, right)*

ANAIS: *(Looking off, left)* Oh no. My husband. Sir, help me!

FADLEY: Here. Quick, put this on.

(FADLEY helps ANAIS into the officer's coat, puts the hat on her head and pulls it low, then places her behind the shrub to hide her skirt and shoes. Enter BEAUPERTHUIS, limping badly.)

BEAUPERTHUIS: So! You thought you could escape me.

FADLEY: No, somehow I knew I couldn't.

BEAUPERTHUIS: These damned shoes slowed me down.
I am armed, sir, and prepared for violence. I demand
that you open your house and allow me to search for
my wife.

FADLEY: Step right in and help yourself. Watch the
stairs, Felix just waxed them this morning.

BEAUPERTHUIS: *(Noticing* ANAIS*)* And who is this? The
wife-thieving soldier!?

FADLEY: No, no. An old friend. Physically, a confirmed
bachelor. *(Confidentially)* He was wounded, sir, in the,
uh…war. Just sharing a laugh. Ha, ha, ha.

*(*FADLEY *gives* ANAIS *a hearty slap on the back. She gives a
deep, throaty laugh.)*

BEAUPERTHUIS: Nobody makes a laughing stock out of
Napoleon P Beauperthuis—not even my wife.

(He exits into the house)

ANAIS: Hide me, sir!

FADLEY: We tried that, remember?

ANAIS: You'll be an accessory to bloodshed! Take pity
on me!

FADLEY: On *you*? My wife has been arrested—on my
wedding day!

ANAIS: I hear him coming!

FADLEY: I don't hear anything.

*(Horrendous CRASH of a large body falling down the stairs.
A beat)*

FADLEY: Now I hear him.

(Enter BEAUPERTHUIS, *painfully.* FADLEY *goes to him.)*

BEAUPERTHUIS: Damn your damnable stairs! And these
shoes! Where is my wife!? I demand an answer!

(Enter, right, EMILE running, with the Italian straw hat. He skids to halt when he sees BEAUPERTHUIS, hides behind a shrub. FADLEY grabs an umbrella from inside the door. He turns BEAUPERTHUIS away with a push to his back.)

FADLEY: *(Pointing him left, opening the umbrella)* Oh no, look at those rain clouds!

BEAUPERTHUIS: What clouds? It's the dark of night!

FADLEY: *(Covering his head with the umbrella)* You'll be soaked to the bone!

(Business: EMILE takes a step toward ANAIS, who reaches out to him dramatically. But each time BEAUPERTHUIS emerges from under the umbrella, EMILE ducks behind the other shrub.)

BEAUPERTHUIS: *(Pushing the umbrella away)* It's not raining!

FADLEY: A cloudburst, any moment!

BEAUPERTHUIS: Let me question that soldier!

FADLEY: In the middle of a deluge?

BEAUPERTHUIS: Will you stop!

FADLEY: If only I could!

(EMILE has now managed to get the hat to ANAIS, take his own coat and hat and sprint off.)

BEAUPERTHUIS: *(Finally pushing free of the umbrella)* I demand the return of my wife!!

(BEAUPERTHUIS turns and sees his wife. She is now wearing the hat. Hands on hips, the angry woman:)

(Sung, operatically:)

ANAIS: So! There you are at last!

BEAUPERTHUIS: Anais.

ANAIS: Napoleon P Beauperthuis, where in the name of decency have you been?

BEAUPERTHUIS: Where have *I* been?

ANAIS: Is this the way you conduct yourself on the streets of New York City, sir? At midnight?

BEAUPERTHUIS: That hat.

FADLEY: She's got the hat.

ANAIS: Do you let your wife make her way home alone after dark? I have been waiting for you since noon at my cousin Eloise's!

BEAUPERTHUIS: Eloise's?

ANAIS: I am outraged, sir, at your behavior!

BEAUPERTHUIS: Now, now just a minute here. You left the house fifteen hours ago to buy a pair of English leather gloves!

(Spoken, as before:)

ANAIS: I changed my mind. I prefer Spanish leather.

BEAUPERTHUIS: But— But what about this horse that ate the hat?

ANAIS: What horse?

FADLEY: What hat?

ANAIS: *(To* FADLEY*)* We have not been introduced, sir.

FADLEY: Fadley, Madam, Winslow C. Say, isn't that a lady's Italian straw hat with fake fruit you're wearing?

ANAIS: Why yes, I believe it is.

FADLEY: Those are hard to come by.

BEAUPERTHUIS: What about the soldier!? What about the woman without the hat!?

FADLEY: Did you see a soldier nearby here, Madam?

ANAIS: Not that I recall.

FADLEY: And you do have a hat.

ANAIS: I should hope so.

BEAUPERTHUIS: But, but, but, but—!!

ANAIS: *(To her husband)* Are you quite through disgracing yourself now? I should like to go home.

(Enter HELEN, *followed by* NONCORT *and* BOBBY*)*

HELEN: Winslow!

NONCORT: Son-in-law!

HELEN: It's heroic!

NONCORT: It's positively vaudevillian!

FADLEY: *(To* BEAUPERTHUIS*)* Sir, may I introduce my wedding party?

NONCORT: We heard the whole story from that soldier—!

(But HELEN *interrupts* NONCORT *with a timely swing of the potted plant into the latter's belly, rendering him at least temporarily speechless)*

HELEN: I have wanted to do that for nineteen years.

FADLEY: Helen, it took me all day, but we're home at last, and our honeymoon suite is finally empty——or ready, I mean. Can you forgive me?

HELEN: Winslow Fadley, swear to me that you're not going to act this weird for the rest of our lives.

FADLEY: I swear it.

HELEN: Good.

(She kisses him. Applause and general approval from the assembly, including the musicians who strike up a tune… Filled with confidence that he has earned the right to sing, FADLEY *goes for it. The others join in, including* ANAIS *and her confused husband. Even* EMILE *makes a tentative entrance, but remains discreetly in the background.)*

 FADLEY: You'd hardly think it credible
 HELEN: A hat his horse found edible

HELEN & FADLEY: Caused such stress

ALL: Nonetheless
We find it rather curious,
A hat can be injurious
To your health.

NONCORT: And my wealth.

HELEN: No, no, no!
This infamous chapeau!
Deliver us from this sombrero!

FADLEY: A journey quite quixotic
Was launched;

HELEN: It was hypnotic
In its scope.

ALL: He gave up hope.
Escaped his place in infamy.
This hat from sunny Italy
Can disappear.

FADLEY: Helen, my dear!

ALL: No, no, no!
This infamous chapeau!
Deliver us from this sombrero!

FADLEY: Adventure quite American,
HELEN: But please let's not go there again.
HELEN & FADLEY: We've had enough,

ALL: This vaudeville stuff!

FADLEY: We botched it all confusingly
HELEN: To please you all amusingly
HELEN & FADLEY: We always strive

ALL: That's vaudeville live!
Go now and thrive!
Don't drink and drive!

(In mid-number, UNCLE FEZ emerges from the townhouse.)

UNCLE FEZ: The hat! That woman has the hat!

(FADLEY *manages to hide* UNCLE FEZ *with the open umbrella, and the song concludes.*)

CHORUS 1:
God save our hat!
Our hat!

CHORUS 2:
Oh folly absolute
To set off in pursuit
Of a lady's hat with fruit!

CHORUS 1:
God save our hat!

CHORUS 2:
What was he thinking of?
When push, it came to shove,
He did it all for love!
FADLEY: I did it all for love!
ALL: Inspired from above
He did! It! All! For love!

(Lights, please)

END OF PLAY